# 30 Day Business Builder Book for Network Marketing Professionals

## Daily Assignments Workbook

Published by Paul G Walmsley.

30 Day Business Builder Book for Network Marketing Professionals: Daily Assignments Workbook.

For more information about this workbook and Paul's first book From HELLO to YES in 3 Minutes or LESS, along with other helpful tools and resources please visit:

www.mytelephonecoachfreeresources.com

Paul G Walmsley-1st ed.

ISBN-13: 978-1499127676

ISBN-10: 1499127677

First Edition

# Praise for the 30 Day Accountability Group and for the 30 Day Business Builder Book for Network Marketing Professionals: Daily Assignments Workbook

"Paul, from the bottom of my heart I want to thank you for blessing each and everyone of us! Your servant leadership has been a beacon for me personally and I know I am a better person than I was 30 days ago!"

– Raelyn Whitney

"I just talked to two people on my CHICKEN LIST and secured two appointments to drop off bottles for each of them! I can honestly say that it has been a direct result of your coaching and that you gave me the courage to make those calls! Thank you, kind sir!"

– Madie Vilbig-King

"Thank you, Paul Walmsley, for being an incredible friend and mentor. We so appreciate you taking your time to help us be successful. You are truly a servant leader."

– Karen Usevitch

"I always wondered how to invite people to my parties. I wrote scripts to say to people, however, since they did not sound right to me, I never made the calls. Now, I can blow up my phone with invites to my parties! And, I never thought of asking, "Who else should we invite?" What a brilliant question!"

– Rajuy Elbey

"Thank you, Paul! This is awesome! I learned and applied so much knowledge!"

– Rosa Andre

"Paul, it goes without saying, but I'm gonna say it anyway, YOU HAVE BEEN AWESOME!"

– Cherie Leffe Goldsmith

"Thank you, Paul, for your great mentorship and for taking the time to work with us and help us be better. This book stares at me in the face every morning and it screams at me, "Now, what are you going to do with this information?" It would be foolish of me to move on without mastering the mundane. Thank you so again and now I am going to SHUT THE HELL UP!"

– Linda Belt

"Thanks Paul, this is excellent. I learn more everyday and I appreciate all that you do."

– Dee Robison

"Thank you, Paul Walmsley. This has been helpful to the 10th degree. I look forward to shaking your hand with gratitude."

– Jeff Golf

"I have said this many times over the last 30 days, I am so grateful for all your wisdom, time and effort. Thank you most sincerely!"

– Madie Vilbig-King

Welcome to the 30 Day Business Builder Book for Network Marketing Professionals. The idea for this book was initiated by a wonderful lady, Anne Lane, who reached out to me January 1, 2014. Anne contacted me and asked for some guidance. When we had finished up, I asked her, "Are you really serious and committed this year?" She replied, "100%, I want it more than air." GAME OVER. After an answer like that, the least I could do was offer to work with Anne for the next 30 days and hold her accountable. She agreed. Later that day I casually posted on Facebook, asking if anyone else would like to join an "Accountability Group." I was astonished by the flood of requests. We started the very next day.

Over the following 30 days lives were changed. Generally I detest that saying because it is used so frequently and frivolously. However, the 422 people in the group went on a journey that really was transformational. As we progressed further and deeper into the 30 days, it became evident that we were really on to something. I have to thank each and every one of the members of the initial group for their contributions ranging from posts, funnies, questions and emotional selfie videos with tears streaming down their faces. Amazing.

The great success of the first group prompted us to start back at the beginning with another group, with over 600 network marketing professionals participating. My hope is that this book will become your go to source for real life useful tips and techniques. Take this book with you wherever you go. You can refer to it for inspiration, reminders, how tos and also as a disciplinary tool to keep you on track. At the back of the book you will find a bonus assignment concerning goals, inventory and planning which can be used at the beginning of the 30 days, in the middle and again at then end. You can refer to this assignment any time you feel a little off kilter. It will help you focus and put you back on course. At the back of the book there are also some extra worksheets and checklists you can print out as you need them.

There is only one rule for the next 30 days. You must complete each assignment, no cherry picking. Go in the order laid out. If you start to fall behind, no big deal, as the saying goes, "Go slow to go fast." Do not get all stressed out if you cannot complete an assignment each day. Take a load off, have a little break and then start right back in refreshed. If you decide to pick and choose which assignments to do, you are doing yourself a disservice. Trust me on this. Use these 30 days as not only a journey to become a better network marketing professional, but also a better person.

My goal is for this 30 Day Business Builder Book to compliment the training provided by network marketing companies. In no way is it designed to undermine any other training or teaching. Please make sure you stop by my website, www.mytelephonecoachfreeresources.com for free goodies to help you on your journey. I can be reached via email at mytelephonecoach@gmail.com. This 30 Day Business Builder Workbook is an organic, growing, developing life-form and I welcome feedback and suggestions from the participants of our accountability group. I would also be tickled pink to receive photos of the workbook as it accompanies you throughout your day, in the coffee shop, on the passenger seat, stuffed in a purse or backpack, pages ragged, notes all over it.

Humbly yours,

Paul G Walmsley

# Table of Contents

# DAY 1: MONDAY
# WHAT IS YOUR WHY?

The most important ingredient in creating success as a network marketing professional is to start with your WHY. To help you with what it means to start with your WHY, watch this 18 minute TEDx talk by Simon Sinek.

http://bit.ly/SimonSinekWHY

Now that you have watched the video, it is time to create your WHY. When someone asks you what you do, you can reply with, "Before I tell you what I do and how I do it, let me share with you WHY I do what I do." Your WHY needs to:

- stop other people in their tracks
- reach into their soul and haunt them the rest of the day because they do not have a WHY like yours
- wake them up and have them tell themselves that they want to be part of what you are doing
- inspire them to be led by you
- get their attention and help you stand out from all the noise

Your WHY will be an ongoing project. You will refer to it daily and refine it as you go.

**Note:** Your WHY should NOT be a WHAT. For example, paying off your debt is a WHAT whereas WHY you want to pay off your debt is to give you peace, freedom and the ability to make better choices for you and your family.

**Exercise 1**

To begin your WHY, start with writing a list of words or phrases that describe what motivates you. This will help you formulate a WHY that is easy to communicate.

**Example:** peace, stress free, not feeling trapped, freedom of choice

## Exercise 2

As you work on your WHY you will actually discover that you need two different WHYS. One WHY is the one that resonates with your very being and it is the one that makes you leap out of bed in the morning and is there for you to fall back on when faced with challenges and setbacks. This WHY can be lengthy, emotional, descriptive and very personal.

Write your WHY:

## Exercise 3

The second WHY is your "elevator speech" kind of WHY. This is the one you share with complete strangers when they ask you what you do. Remember, when out prospecting for people to join your organization, you want to have a very focused and inspiring WHY so that the person on the other end of it decides right there and then (although they may not fully realize it immediately) that they want to join you, be a part of your cause and be led by you. You can use a couple of formulas to help you with your elevator speech WHY.

## Formula:

I was_____ _____ Then I discovered
_____ and now I
_____.
That's WHY I now_____ and it gives
me_____.

**Example:** I was _stuck in a rut, facing a midlife crisis, and wondering where my life was going._ Then I discovered _this amazing company_ and now _I leap out of bed in the morning. I love working towards my dreams and goals each day._

That's WHY I now help other people who are in the same position as I was, turn their lives around. _It gives me an_ unbelievable sense of achievement and I just love being there for them.

**Try a few of these:**

I was

_____

Then I discovered

_____

and now I

_____

That's WHY I now

_____

and it gives me

_____

I was

_____

Then I discovered

_____

and now I

_____

That's WHY I now

_____

and it gives me

_____

I was

_____

Then I discovered

_____

and now I

_____

That's WHY I now

_____

and it gives me

_____

**Here's a second formula you could use:**

I help X achieve Y, even if Z. And as a result, benefit #1, benefit #2, benefit #3, which is WHY I do what I do.

**Example:** I help stay at home moms earn an extra $500 – $1000 per month and drive a free ................ even if they have never done this kind of thing before. The incredible boost to their confidence, (benefit #1) the reduction of their stress (benefit #2) and the transformation of their demeanor (benefit #3) is a thrill for me. I love being there to help them. That is why I do what I do.

**Work on a few examples using this formula:**

I help _____

achieve/gain/become/earn _____

even if they _____

The _____ (benefit #1)

_____ (benefit #2)

and _____ (benefit #3)

is a real _____ for me and I love being there to help them. That is WHY I do what I do.


I help _____

achieve/gain/become/earn _____

even if they _____

The _____ (benefit #1)

_____ (benefit #2)

and _____ (benefit #3)

is a real _____ for me and I love being there to help them. That is WHY I do what I do.


I help _____

achieve/gain/become/earn _____

even if they _____

The _____ (benefit #1)

_____ (benefit #2)

and _____ (benefit #3)

is a real _____ to me and I love

being there to help them. That is WHY I do what I do.


Now, use your personal WHY to create your "elevator speech"
WHY:

_____

_____

_____

_____

_____

_____

_____

_____

_____

_____

_____

_____

_____

_____

---

---

---

Now, rewrite your personal WHY:

---

---

---

---

---

---

---

---

---

---

---

---

---

---

---

---

---

**Bonus Tip #1**

Put your elevator speech WHY on the back of your business card. Keep the front of your business card very clean. Less is more. Whenever you hand your business card to people, hand it to them with your WHY face up. When they read your WHY and ask who you work for, tell them to turn it over. Try to avoid listing product features and benefits, this gives the game away.

# Notes

_____

_____

_____

_____

_____

_____

_____

_____

_____

_____

_____

_____

_____

_____

_____

_____

_____

_____

_____

_____

_____

_____

_____

# DAY 2: TUESDAY
# WRITE YOUR LIST

Every successful business begins with a strong foundation and as a network marketing professional your rock, your foundation upon which everything is built, is your list of prospects. Let's get started with laying the foundations with your INITIAL list. Remember, do not make the mistake of pre-judging anyone.

**"If you know they exist, they go on your list."**

**Exercise 4**

Write down all the contacts in your:

- phone
- Facebook
- high School
- grade School
- past jobs, etc.

Write down all the names of everyone you know even if you only have the person's name and no way to contact them (yet), but you know you want to talk to them. Go!

**Exercise 5**

Think about where you go every day, what you spend your money on (follow your money) and where you are when you present your credit/debit card. Think about the immediate people who serve you and the owners of the establishments, the staff, the suppliers, and other customers associated with each venue. For example, when you go to pick up your dry cleaning, how many names can you remember?

- the staff member(s)
- the owner(s)
- the delivery driver(s)
- the other customers
- the suppliers
- professional staff such as CPA, insurance guy etc.

The possibilities are endless! The goal for you is to have an active, organic, growing, living and breathing list of 1000 prospects at all times. For today, aim for a minimum of 200. In terms of organizing your list, you can be as old school (index cards or notebook) all the way to as high tech as an app or Customer Relationship Management (CRM) software. Do whichever method is the most comfortable for you. This is not the time to learn something or spend a day searching the web for the latest CRM method.

So go on, switch off all distraction, no, I mean it. Get your head down and start writing and thinking and writing and thinking and don't stop until your hand cramps up and your butt is numb.

**Exercise 6**

Number of contacts in your phone _____

Number of Facebook friends _____

Number of Twitter followers _____

Number of LinkedIn connections _____

Number of Pinterest followers _____

Number of _____

Number of _____

Number of _____

Total _____

# Notes

# DAY 3: WEDNESDAY EXPAND YOUR LIST

On Day 2, I asked you to start laying the foundation of your business by writing a list of all your prospects. I asked you to write EVERYONE down, "If you know they exist, they are on the list."

**Exercise 7**

Today, go through your list and stop at every single name and ask yourself which two people could that person lead you to? Think about each name on your list and don't move on to the next name until you have written the names of two people that the person knows that you know they know.

For example, I have a friend Danny. I know he has a twin brother and a sister who is big in another network marketing company. I know he knows them...does that make sense?

Danny: His twin brother _____

His sister _____

Progress down the list and again, do not skip any names, think deep and hard if necessary, but for pointers, think of their family, who they work with and who they hang out with. So, this little exercise has effectively tripled your list...want to go through the roof? Want to triple the list again? Ok, here goes...

## Exercise 8

Now, go back to the top of the list and start with your original person. You have come up with two people who you know they know. Now come up with two people that you know they know but you don't know.

Huh?

In my example above, I came up with Danny. Then I came up with Danny's twin brother and his sister. I also know he works out at a very upmarket gym and bought a Range Rover recently. So there you go, I am going to add the person who signed him up for his gym membership and the person who sold him his Range Rover. Bam!

All I need to do now is ask Danny for those two names, ask his permission to contact them and use him as a reference and I have now blown my list through the roof with this simple technique.

Danny

1. His twin brother

2. His sister

3. The gym salesperson

4. The guy who sold him the Range Rover.

If you originally started with 200 people on your list and you carried out these simple exercises, you now have an additional 800 people on your list making a total of 1000 people as your foundation. Now, don't start talking yourself out of a bunch of these people just trust me on this and take a couple of minutes to bask in the warm fuzziness of now knowing you have 1000 PEOPLE ON YOUR LIST!

**Exercise 9**

Your total number at the end of exercise 6 _____

Number of people added in exercise 7 _____

Number of people added in exercise 8 _____

Total number of people currently on your list _____

# Notes

# DAY 4: THURSDAY
# GET IN TOUCH
# WITH...YOURSELF

Today is a day off for you. A catch up day to just quiet yourself, find some time for yourself, switch off the phone and the computer and just think. You may be a little overawed at this stage. We have had three very intense assignments so far. But let's take a look at your progress:

Write down your personal WHY again here:

_____

_____

_____

_____

_____

_____

_____

_____

_____

_____

_____

_____

_____


Write down your 30-60 second elevator speech WHY that you deliver when someone asks what you do:

_____

_____

_____

_____

_____

_____

_____

_____

_____

_____

_____


Total number of people currently on your list _____

By now you really should be feeling much more confident about your business. You have nailed why the heck you are even doing this business and you now have a list of at least 1000 people. Enjoy the rest of the day off....if you can take your mind off all of this that is!

# Notes

_____

_____

_____

_____

_____

_____

_____

_____

_____

_____

_____

_____

_____

_____

_____

_____

_____

_____

_____

_____

_____

_____

# DAY 5: FRIDAY
# THE 5 SECOND RULE

The 5 Second Rule comes into play when you consider approaching someone about your business opportunity or the products that you market. This could be in the line at the grocery store, having eye contact at the coffee shop, or looking at your list and contemplating a person to call.

So, you are at the coffee shop and someone next to you grabs your attention. Maybe you've even exchanged some pleasantries....then The 5 Second Rule kicks in. You have 5 seconds to either talk yourself into approaching that person OR 5 seconds to talk yourself out of it. I am sure you can relate, we have all been there. This is one of the reasons why we have focused so much on our WHY.

As The 5 Second Rule kicks in, I want you to immediately think of your WHY and ask yourself, "Will approaching this person right here, right now, bring me closer to my WHY?" You know the answer. Approach them.

## Exercise 10

Get out there amongst the public and recognize The 5 Second Rule happening. Then, commit to approaching more people. Get uncomfortable, but grow.

## Exercise 11

Then, once you have recognized The 5 Second Rule kicking in, refer to your WHY and then approach the person in your sight. Do this AT LEAST TWICE today and then note down the outcomes, not only how the approach went, but your feelings as The 5 Second Rule came into affect, how you worked through it and then how you felt once you had approached the prospect.

**Example:**

What you felt during The 5 Second Rule:

*She looks super confident and seems very outgoing, but she is probably too busy and is successful in whatever she is currently doing.*

How you overcame it:

*I asked myself if having her on my team would help me achieve my why.*

How did you approach them?

*I offered her my business card.*

Outcome of the approach:

_I gained her contact information and she agreed to read an email I would send later tonight._

## Prospect # 1

What you felt during The 5 Second Rule:

_____

_____

_____

_____

How you overcame it:

_____

_____

_____

_____

How did you approach them?

_____

_____

_____

_____

Outcome of the approach:

_____

_____

_____

_____

## Prospect # 2

What you felt during The 5 Second Rule:

_____

_____

_____

_____

How you overcame it:

_____

_____

_____

_____

How did you approach them?

_____

_____

_____

_____

Outcome of the approach:

_____

_____

_____

_____

# Notes

_____

_____

_____

_____

_____

_____

_____

_____

_____

_____

_____

_____

_____

_____

_____

_____

_____

_____

_____

_____

_____

_____

# DAY 6: SATURDAY BACK TO THE LIST...TRUST ME!

Professional network marketers refer to their lists as being "active" because EACH DAY they add to it. You have been building your list and adding to it. Today's assignment is super simple. Count up your list and add another fifty to the total. Don't skimp, do all fifty. There are twenty five days left in this project, and with the fifty new contacts you write down today, you will have two people you need to contact each day.

Don't worry about how you will contact them yet. Just add to your list. Then plot and plan how you will contact every single person on your list by the end of these thirty days. Now, if your WHY is big enough you'll do this. If it is not, you either need to REFINE YOU WHY or accept that you are not truly committed to it.

Here is a little thought provoker: if you have kids, go back through the last year and recollect each and every birthday party you either attended with them or dropped them off at. Then, think of the owners and/or managers of the establishment. Would they be interested in an extra income source? Would they have a readymade list of prospects? Of course they would, so put them on your list!

Then, think of the people who attend all these birthday parties. Not only the people themselves, but who would they know? Who could they lead you to? When you think like this, another 50 names should be a piece of (birthday) cake!

# Notes

_____

_____

_____

_____

_____

_____

_____

_____

_____

_____

_____

_____

_____

_____

_____

_____

_____

_____

_____

_____

_____

_____

_____

# DAY 7: SUNDAY
# DON'T FREAK OUT BUT…

I want you to stop entirely posting ANY direct information about your products and opportunity on Facebook for three, YES THREE, entire days!

"Holy crap, has Paul lost it?" I hear you bellow.

## Exercise 12

Remove all of your marketing collateral from your page. There should be NO logos, NO before and afters, NO company announcements, and NO product references. Make sure your Facebook banner expresses YOUR PERSONALITY and your profile photo reminds people of who YOU are.

## Exercise 13

Read every post that appears from your friends on your news feed and look for opportunities to reach out and contact them, WITHOUT mentioning products or opportunities. I don't give a flying you-know-what if there is a major announcement or event coming up. What I want you to do is unleash your personality back onto your page. Reveal things about yourself, post some funny shit, maybe some useful stuff, why not even post some nice things about your friends? The opportunities are endless. Go on, have some fun with this and at the same time just read about your friends, listen to them, observe them, appreciate them and fall back in love with them. Look for their highs, their lows, their successes and their challenges.

Be there for them, care for them and provide each and every one of them with a gift. It might be a LIKE, a SHARE, a COMMENT or even a PRIVATE MESSAGE. Send them a reminder of who you both are, maybe an old photo, recall a memory, bring up a funny from your past, be creative and make them smile. Ask them a question so that they say to themselves, "You know what? No one has EVER asked me a question like that before." And then LISTEN.

## Exercise 14

List 3 things you learned about your friends.

Example: Dave has gotten really involved in jiu jitsu.

1._____

_____

_____

2._____

_____

3._____

_____

_____

Describe three of your own posts that gained the most likes/shares/comments.

**Example:** The joke I posted about wanting to be an alpha male.

1._____

_____

_____

2._____

_____

_____

3._____

_____

_____

Describe the three posts that you noticed from your friends that gained the most likes/shares/comments

**Example:** Funny viral animal video from Sue.

1._____

_____

_____

2._____

_____

_____

3._____

_____

_____

What conclusions can you draw from this exercise?

**Example:** When my friends post a funny quote or photo they get a lot of likes because they are entertaining and demonstrate their personality.

1._____

_____

_____

2._____

_____

_____

3._____

_____

_____

Hopefully you have now discovered that FB is not simply a medium for throwing up all over your friends about your business and your products. Instead, it is a way to connect, entertain, care for and be there for your friends. Never forget that. There is nothing wrong with posting about your business and your products, but follow the simple formula from Gary Vaynerchuk's latest book, "Jab, Jab, Jab, Right Hook." (Give, Give, Give, Ask)

# Notes

_____

_____

_____

_____

_____

_____

_____

_____

_____

_____

_____

_____

_____

_____

_____

_____

_____

_____

_____

_____

_____

_____

# DAY 8: MONDAY USE FORM TO BUILD RAPPORT

I hope going "cold turkey" when it comes to Facebook hasn't been too tough on you. Guess what though, you still have 2 FULL DAYS LEFT! That's right, the assignment was to stay away from products and opportunity posts for 3 DAYS not just the one. Can you do it? WILL you do it? Today's assignment is all about using a simple formula to build rapport and ask good questions. The formula is FORM.

**FAMILY**

**OCCUPATION**

**RECREATION**

**MOTIVATION**

Whenever you are striking up any kind of conversation with someone be it Belly to Belly, over the telephone or via social media, use FORM to give you a framework. FORM will eliminate awkward silences and give you confidence. Asking open questions concerning those four topics will invariably help the other person relax and open up to you.

FORM will not only help you build rapport, but also identify potential problems the other person may have. After all, we are in the problem solving business, aren't we? In a future assignment, we will cover in depth how to use another formula to reveal the golden nugget we are searching for. But for now, as you conduct your two exposures today, experiment with different questions you can use for each topic.

**Exercise 15**

Write two ideas of questions you can ask for each topic.

**FAMILY**

Example: "So, how's the family?"

1._____

_____

2._____

_____


**OCCUPATION**

Example: "How's work?"

1._____

_____

2._____

_____

## RECREATION

Example: "Anything fun planned for the weekend?"

1._____

_____

2._____

_____

## MOTIVATION

Example: "So how are you feeling? What's going on?"

1._____

_____

2._____

_____

You can use FORM in other ways as well, it just provides a very clear and simple path to follow. For example, when I delivered my dad's eulogy I used FORM. I practiced and practiced and did not need any notes because to me it made sense. I started the eulogy describing dad's family, I then summarised his career, I shared with everyone what he liked to do in his spare time and I finished off the eulogy describing the kind of man he was and just what made him tick.

# Notes

_____

_____

_____

_____

_____

_____

_____

_____

_____

_____

_____

_____

_____

_____

_____

_____

_____

_____

_____

_____

_____

# DAY 9: TUESDAY PROBLEM IDENTIFY, PROBLEM AGITATE, PROBLEM SOLVE

"What the heck is Paul on about now? Not another thing I have to remember, when will it all end?" I know this is what you are muttering to yourself right now. But, if you stay with me you will see how all of this will fall into place and you will be a successful business builder! So, we've noticed someone in the coffee shop, overcome The 5 Second Rule and gone over to them and have built some rapport with them using FORM. Now, we move on to the next part of our system.

I want you to have the posture of a professional, as a consultant, as a problem solver, as a mentor, not a predator, not an ambulance chaser, not someone who is desperate, someone who is under pressure to hit some kind of sales goal. So, as you use FORM, you need to IDENTIFY A PROBLEM, such as not liking their job, not making enough money, not having enough time with their family, not feeling fulfilled, no time for fun, feeling trapped in the rat race, etc. Then you want to AGITATE

THE PROBLEM. What I mean by that is, have the person describe in more detail what they meant when they revealed their problem, such as: "I'm sorry to hear that you are not enjoying your job, what's going on? What's the most frustrating part of it?"

Practice your own questions, your own way of peeling the layers of the onion back. Spend time with them, listen to them, reach out to them, show you care about them. Have them tell you about what is really getting to them. When they start to open up, let them go. Do not interrupt at all! Let it all pour out. Keep yourself out of the way.

You will be tempted to immediately jump in when they reveal a problem and blab about your company, but don't. Take your time. Then, once they have surprised themselves by just how much they have revealed you now OFFER THE SOLUTION.

"Wow, you know what, I may have a way to help..."

"Sorry to hear that, maybe my company and the team of leaders I work could help..."

"Gosh, I just thought about something....maybe my company could make a difference..."

THEN SHUT THE HELL UP and let them ask you what the heck you are talking about. Guess what, you just PIQUED THEIR INTEREST!

**Exercise 16**

List some questions to help you identify a potential problem:

**FAMILY**

Example: How's the family doing? Do you get enough time with your kids? Missed any major events recently due to work?

1._____

_____

_____

_____

2._____

_____

_____

_____

3._____

_____

_____

_____

**OCCUPATION**

Example: Still enjoying work? How much personal development

training does your company provide? What kind of leadership or mentoring is provided for you? Do you have a clear path ahead for the next 3-5 years, has your boss sat down with you to help you plan it all out?

1._____

_____

_____

_____

2._____

_____

_____

_____

3._____

_____

_____

_____

## RECREATION

Example: Any new hobbies? How much free time do you get each week? What sort of things would you do if you had more time on your hands?

1._____

_____

_____

_____

2._____

_____

_____

_____

3._____

_____

_____

_____

## MOTIVATION

Example: How are you feeling? Are you more or less optimistic than last year at this time? What drives you? What pissed you off? What scares you?

1._____

_____

_____

2._____

_____

_____

_____

3._____

_____

_____

_____


**Exercise 17**

List some questions that will help you agitate the problem.

**Example:** I am sorry to hear that you don't have enough time for soccer anymore, how many times a week did you used to play?

1._____

_____

_____

_____

2._____

_____

_____

_____

3._____

_____

_____

_____

In Day 10 we are going to lead into a way of solving the problems you have just uncovered and agitated with your business opportunity.

# Notes

_____

_____

_____

_____

_____

_____

_____

_____

_____

_____

_____

_____

_____

_____

_____

_____

_____

_____

_____

_____

_____

_____

# DAY 10: WEDNESDAY PIQUE INTEREST WITHOUT MENTIONING PRODUCT/COMPANY (PROBLEM SOLVE)

*Side note: This is your first day after the three days of cold turkey from posting about your business and opportunities. DO NOT waste the three days by unleashing and dumping on FB about your products and business.*

Take all of the above that we have worked on so far, grab a bunch of people from your list, find at least two more prospects that are right now complete strangers and then PIQUE INTEREST with them without mentioning the product or the company.

"Huh?"

By staying away from your company name and its products, that will force you to really work on crafting your words and approach, especially the questions you are going to ask. In my regular job, the product is a formality as I am writing up the order. I don't lead with the product, it is the final thing they hear about. By then, I have identified their problem(s), agitated the you-know-what out of them and then simply put my arm around them (while on the telephone on the opposite side of the country) and offered the solution using the products I sell.

So, restrain yourself, test yourself, challenge yourself to be able to overcome The 5 Second Rule, build rapport using FORM, identify a problem, agitate that problem, and propose that you may have a possible solution to their problem without having mentioned your company or its products.

Phew!

Now, how do you pique interest in your company or your products and never mention either?

**Exercise 18**

List some questions or comments you would use to link into your possible solution.

Example: "You know what? I just thought of something, my company helps people overcome that..."

Example: "Gosh, I just realized, I may just have the solution for that..."

1._____

_____

_____

_____

2._____

_____

_____

_____

3._____

_____

_____

_____

4._____

_____

_____

_____

5._____

_____

_____

_____

6._____

_____

_____

_____

Imagine how confident you will feel knowing that I could literally drop you off in any town or city in the country and instantly you could start growing a business with complete strangers. Now, that's gold right there.

# Notes

_____

_____

_____

_____

_____

_____

_____

_____

_____

_____

_____

_____

_____

_____

_____

_____

_____

_____

_____

_____

_____

_____

# DAY 11: THURSDAY
# DAY OFF
# RECHARGE & CATCH UP

As we did last week, I am going to give you today off, let you recharge and catch up. By now, hopefully, you will have seen improvements in your skill set, mindset and confidence. If we ended the program here, hopefully it will have been worth it. We are only about a third of the way through! So, it is probably tough going at the moment keeping up. I have probably given you too much already. However, this is the crucial time.

This is when you take stock and assess how far you have come and then roll up your sleeves to take it up another gear. But for today, just take a breather. Call someone you haven't spoken to in at least three years and just say "Hi." Don't you dare bring up the business!

**Exercise 19**

Do a quick inventory of where you are with your business. Assess your strength and your weaknesses. List the opportunities you have before you and also the threats to you being a massive success.

## Strengths

Example: <u>I can confidently approach anybody with a smile on my face.</u>

1._____

_____

_____

2._____

_____

_____

3._____

_____

_____

4._____

_____

_____

5._____

_____

_____

## Weaknesses

**Example:** I take rejection too personally.

1._____

_____

_____

2._____

_____

_____

3._____

_____

_____

4._____

_____

_____

5._____

_____

_____

## Opportunities

**Example:** In my neighborhood are many retailers that I can approach.

1._____

_____

2._____

_____

_____

3._____

_____

_____

4._____

_____

_____

5._____

_____

_____

**Threats**

**Example:** Somebody else may approach someone on my list before I do.

1._____

_____

_____

2._____

_____

_____

3._____

_____

_____

4._____

_____

_____

5._____

_____

_____

Finally, turn to someone you love, give them a kiss, scratch behind their ear, tickle their belly and tell them how much they mean to you.

# Notes

_____

_____

_____

_____

_____

_____

_____

_____

_____

_____

_____

_____

_____

_____

_____

_____

_____

_____

_____

_____

_____

_____

# DAY 12: FRIDAY
# 3RD PARTY TOOLS

Time to get down to business and focus on the use of 3rd Party Tools. Let's just cover why the use of 3rd Party Tools is so important. It is all about DUPLICATION. When you are in front of a prospect, NEVER ANSWER YOUR OWN PROSPECT'S QUESTIONS, instead present them with a 3rd Party Tool. As the saying goes, "If your lips are moving, your fingers should be pointing." (At a 3rd Party Tool.)

Why? Well, again, it's all about duplication. You want the person on the other end of the question to watch a video, read a magazine, listen to a CD, visit your website, jump on a call, attend an event, etc. That way, the person thinks to themselves, "Well, that was easy! Paul didn't give me a sales pitch, he didn't have to memorize some kind of presentation, in fact he didn't even answer any of my questions. All he did was give me a DVD to watch….I CAN DO THAT!"

BAM!

**Exercise 20**

Take inventory of the different 3rd Party Tools you have available. Assess each one and figure which ones would best fit each scenario and prospect.List the 3rd Party tools you have available and outline who they would be suitable for and when/how you would use them:

**Example:**

Tool: Magazine

Suitable for: Females I bump into in the cold market

How would you use it: I would keep a supply in my car and when I approach someone, once I feel that they could be a good prospect, I would run out to my car and get one.

Tool: _____

Suitable for:

_____

How would you use it:

_____

_____

_____

Tool: _____

Suitable for:

_____

How would you use it:

_____

_____

_____


Tool: _____

Suitable for:

_____

How would you use it:

_____

_____

_____


Tool:_____

Suitable

for:_____

How would you use it:

_____

_____

_____

Tool: _____

Suitable

for:_____

How would you use it:

_____

_____

_____


Tool: _____

Suitable for:

_____

How would you use it:

_____

_____

_____


Tool:_____

Suitable

for:_____


How would you use it:

_____

_____

_____

Tool: _____

Suitable for:

_____

How would you use it:

_____

_____

_____

Tool: _____

Suitable for:

_____

How would you use it:

_____

_____

_____

Tool: _____

Suitable for:

_____

How would you use it:

_____

_____

_____

Undoubtedly, you will have your "favorite" or "go to" 3rd Party Tools and that's OK. However, don't get complacent. Mix it up a bit and test different tools in different scenarios with different kinds of prospects. You're a pro right? Well go ahead and act like a pro. Please don't just use a magazine a handful of times and then discard it as not being useful just because it didn't recruit you a whale. You are smarter than that right?

Cool.

# Notes

_____

_____

_____

_____

_____

_____

_____

_____

_____

_____

_____

_____

_____

_____

_____

_____

_____

_____

_____

_____

_____

_____

# DAY 13: SATURDAY
# HOW TO BUTTON DOWN THE 3rd PARTY TOOL, SCHEDULE THE FOLLOW UP & LAY DOWN THE FOUNDATION FOR A 3 WAY CALL

Now that you have completed a full inventory of the 3rd Party Tools you have at your disposal and given consideration as to how and who with you want to deploy them, you now need to work on the actual presentation/delivery of them. As always, we have a game plan and a formula. The game plan is that we never answer our own recruit's questions, instead we use the most appropriate and suitable 3rd Party Tool to do all the work.

Let's recap again why. The whole basis of recruiting for your organization is that you want the potential recruit to see how easy it is to present the product and/or the opportunity. I know we have covered this before, but it is crucial that you get this embedded into your head. Otherwise, when a prospect asks a decent question, you'll answer it and then the floodgates open.

Then, 45 minutes later when both you and the prospect are exhausted, you'll be looking desperate and they'll be looking for the door!

So, discipline yourself and as soon as your prospects issues a belter such as,

"Well, does this stuff actually work?" You can answer along the lines of, "That's a great question, Joe. As a matter of fact, the company provides a number of resources to help answer that question..."

**Exercise 21**

Introduce your chosen 3rd Party Tool by USING A FORMULA:

"If I COULD...,
WOULD you...?
WHEN can I...?
BECAUSE..."

Example: "If I could send you an email with a link to a video on my website, would you watch it? Great, when can I follow up to see what you liked best? OK, Tuesday morning. Wonderful, because we have a big event coming up next Saturday and you may decide you want to be there once you've watched the video."

**Example:**

Link/Segue response

That's a great question _____

As a matter of fact, the company provides a number of resources to help answer that question

If I COULD get you a magazine with a DVD inside

WOULD you take 15 minutes to read and watch it?

WHEN can I pick it back up though?

BECAUSE I have a number of people wanting to get their hands on it too.


**1. Link/Segue response**

_____

_____

_____

_____


If I COULD

_____

_____

WOULD you

_____

_____

WHEN can I

_____

_____

BECAUSE

_____

_____

**2. Link/Segue response**

_____

_____

_____

_____

If I COULD

_____

_____

WOULD you

_____

_____

WHEN can I

_____

_____

BECAUSE

_____

_____

## 3. Link/Segue response

_____

_____

_____

_____

If I COULD

_____

_____

WOULD you

_____

_____

WHEN can I

_____

_____

BECAUSE

_____

_____

## 4. Link/Segue response

_____

_____

_____

_____

If I COULD

_____

_____

WOULD you

_____

_____

WHEN can I

_____

_____

BECAUSE

_____

_____

Practice using this formula. It will help you button down your 3rd Party Tool and solidify a follow up. Don't veer from the formula, don't try your own thing, don't leave a piece of it out. Practice and master this. It is so powerful.

**Bonus Tip #2**

By the way, how do you fancy a little one liner to set up the perfect 3 way call?

Before you end the conversation with your prospect, drop this little gem in there:

"Oh, by the way, when I circle back on Tuesday morning to pick up the magazine you'll probably have some questions. I'll do my best to have Amber available for us, she's great. I love learning from her and I am sure she will be of help."

Not only have you introduced Amber (the prospect will be less defensive now when you offer to call her on the follow up) but you have also laid down the gauntlet that the prospect had better have some questions ready for you. Freakin' genius, even though I say it myself!

So, your assignment today is to present two prospects with your chosen 3rd Party Tool, have them commit to reading/watching/listening to it, have them agree to a specific follow up time and let them know you are going to do your darndest to have _____ available to answer their questions. Go get 'em!

# Notes

# DAY 14: SUNDAY
# HOW TO DOUBLE OR TRIPLE YOUR PROSPECTS WITH A SIMPLE QUESTION

If you practice, master and always use this little technique, this will easily at least double the number of prospects you are working with. Yes, I did say that right, I am going to show you right here and right now how to DOUBLE the number of prospects you have available. Ready?

You've worked the system so far like the professional you are. You have piqued interest and introduced the idea of presenting the prospect with a 3rd Party Tool in order to satisfy their interest and/or answer their question(s). Now use this, each time and every time from now on.

"OK Jenny, I'll stop by tomorrow morning at 11am with the magazine. It's a beautiful magazine with lots of useful stories and tips about _____ and it will answer most of your questions about the product (or business opportunity). By the way....WHO ELSE SHOULD WE GIVE ONE TO?"

What? Did we just ask who WE (yes, you are right, we are now in this together, we are already on the same team) should give another magazine to?

So, let me get this straight, as soon as your prospect comes up with "my mum/sister/neighbor/nanny/workout buddy," not only have you at least DOUBLED your number of prospects, but you have also got your prospect now buying into the system and her wheels are already turning! So, get yourself round there with an extra magazine and use this again and again. You can also use this if you have agreed to meet someone to do a sit down and watch a short video on your iPad.

"Hey, by the way, when we meet at the coffee shop tomorrow, who else should WE invite? Well, who else do you know whose opinion you respect and may also be looking for another five paychecks a month….?"

Did you notice that little belter there at the end? What is the last thing you left percolating in your prospect's mind? Five paychecks a month! Now, if that doesn't pique their interest and solidify the sit down nothing will!

# Notes

_____

_____

_____

_____

_____

_____

_____

_____

_____

_____

_____

_____

_____

_____

_____

_____

_____

_____

_____

_____

_____

_____

# DAY 15: MONDAY
# WE ALL LOVE A GOOD SELFIE

Take out your phone, record a 30-60 second video of yourself talking about what you have gotten from the project so far. Post the video on our group FB page. Thank you for participating!!

# Notes

_____

_____

_____

_____

_____

_____

_____

_____

_____

_____

_____

_____

_____

_____

_____

_____

_____

_____

_____

_____

_____

_____

# DAY 16: TUESDAY
# THE FORTUNE IS IN THE
# FOLLOW UP

I am absolutely amazed how often people drop the ball when it comes to following up. They've done all the hard work of identifying a prospect, overcoming The 5 Second Rule, generating rapport using FORM, identified a problem, agitated it and then offered a potential solution. Then when it comes to following up after exposure to a 3rd Party Tool, a 3 way call or a live event, the follow up is often very weak and sometimes non existent.

And I am no different!

Here is a great example of a poor follow up. Last week, as I was unloading some things from the back of my SUV, one of my neighbors, a super hot Brazilian girl arrived home and parked in the spot next to me. The 5 Second Rule kicked in and because I am accountable to you all now, I went for it. I simply asked if she would like to try this new night cream. I kind of caught her off guard and she kind of quickly said yes she would. As we got in the elevator together she said, "You know I work for a Beverly Hills plastic surgeon don't you?" To which I replied, "No, I didn't. What kind of plastic surgery?" She replied, "face." I was both excited and intimidated. She stopped at my apartment which was on the way to hers and I gave her a dvd to watch and very rushed instructions on how to apply the product, then thrust the bottle into her hand.

I followed up the next day to offer her the day cream and her mom answered the door. She was super excited, so I loaned her a bottle too. Today I had every intention of stopping by to follow up when I bumped into her again. When I asked her what she liked most about the product, she replied, "Oh, I haven't started to use it yet, I haven't had the time."

Gutted, frustrated and kicking myself!

## Exercise 22

So, what lessons can we learn from this catalogue of errors? List all the classic mistakes I made and then offer a better way for me (and you) to execute next time.

## Example:

Mistake: Rushed approach, not pre-planned.

Alternative Approach: I should have built rapport first then requested to stop by later with a product that might have interested her.

Mistake:_____

_____

_____

Alternative Approach:

_____

_____

_____


Mistake:_____

_____

_____

Alternative Approach:

_____

_____

_____


Mistake:_____

_____

_____

Alternative Approach:

_____

_____

_____

Mistake:_____

_____

_____

Alternative Approach:

_____

_____

_____

Mistake:_____

_____

_____

Alternative Approach:

_____

_____

_____

Mistake:_____

_____

_____

Alternative Approach:

_____

_____

_____

Mistake:_____

_____

_____

Alternative Approach:

_____

_____

_____

# Notes

# DAY 17: WEDNESDAY
# 10 PEOPLE

This is a Business Builder Book and not just a nice and easy workbook to half ass fill out when you get an urge now and then. Each day I give assignments in a specific order for specific reasons. I want to make sure you understand why I am doing this and what I expect.

I am providing a very clear path to follow with specific instructions and guidelines. These are not just thoughts or whims, these are battle tested and proven to work. I do not want you to look at each assignment and decide on whether or not you are going to give it a go for a day. No, that's not what this Business Builder Book is about.

This Business Builder Book is for people who are committed and want to be held accountable each day for their efforts in carrying out every assignment. If you decide to just pick the assignments that are the easiest or most palpable, you will not grow. I want you to really stretch yourself, have blind faith in what I am asking you to do and then with all of your heart go out there and do it to the best of your ability.

The 5 Second Rule has been career changing for me. Printing my WHY on the back of my business cards has already started to come to fruition. Just being able to look at someone and then convince myself that this person I am looking at right here, right now could well be my first million dollar earner has been incredible. So, grab today's assignment by the scruff of the neck and work it.

## Exercise 23

1. Add to your list a minimum of 10 new people today.

2. Decide upon and execute how you will approach these 10 new people.

E.g. phone call, Belly to Belly, email, text, FB private message, etc.

3. Then, as soon as you get a response, as soon as interest has been piqued and a question asked, 3 way them to a leader in your organization.

## Example:

New Person: Neighbor Joe

Approach: Belly to Belly

Question they asked: I don't know anything about skin cream, how could I be successful with this?

Leader that took the 3 way: *John*

Outcome: *He is coming to Tuesday's event to learn more and meet other men who have been successful without prior knowledge of the product.*

1. New Person:

_____

_____

Approach:_____

_____

Question they asked:

_____

Leader that took the 3 way:

_____

Outcome:_____

_____

2. New Person:

_____

_____

Approach:_____

_____

Question they asked:

_____

Leader that took the 3 way:

_____

Outcome:_____

_____

3. New Person:

_____

_____

Approach:_____

_____

Question they asked:

_____

Leader that took the 3 way:

_____

Outcome:_____

_____

4. New Person:

_____

_____

Approach:_____

_____

Question they asked:

_____

Leader that took the 3 way:

_____

Outcome:_____

_____

5. New Person:

_____

_____

Approach:_____

_____

Question they asked:

_____

Leader that took the 3 way:

_____

Outcome:_____

_____

6. New Person:

_____

_____

Approach:_____

_____

Question they asked:

_____

Leader that took the 3 way:

_____

Outcome:_____

_____


7. New Person:

_____

_____

Approach:_____

_____

Question they asked:

_____

Leader that took the 3 way:

_____

Outcome:_____

8. New Person:

_____

_____

Approach: _____

_____

Question they asked:

_____

Leader that took the 3 way:

_____

Outcome:_____

_____

9. New Person:

_____

_____

Approach:_____

_____

Question they asked:

_____

Leader that took the 3 way:

_____

Outcome:_____

_____


10. New Person:

_____

_____

Approach:_____

_____

Question they asked:

_____

Leader that took the 3 way:

_____

Outcome:_____

_____


DO NOT STOP TODAY UNTIL 10 PEOPLE HAVE ASKED YOU A QUESTION ABOUT YOUR BUSINESS. And that's it. No explanations of the product, the comp plan, the leadership, the system, the industry, the culture of the company. No, add people to your list, pique their interest and put them on a 3 way call. No more, no less. Imagine mastering this little system, teaching your leaders and then teaching them how to teach it.

# Notes

_____

_____

_____

_____

_____

_____

_____

_____

_____

_____

_____

_____

_____

_____

_____

_____

_____

_____

_____

_____

_____

# DAY 18: THURSDAY
# 3 WAY TO PAY DAY

Let's get right into the nitty gritty. All of you fight the 3 way call...I know, weird how I know, isn't it? You know how I know? My phone is not blowing up with requests for 3 ways and neither are yours from your team. Let me see if I can put to bed the weirdness and icky feeling about 3 way calls.

You are talking to a prospect and it seems to be going well. Your dobber is up and you think you might have one here. You have this little battle going on in the back of your mind...."I'm supposed to get this person on a 3 way, but what if they don't want to? What if my expert isn't available? What if my expert blows it? You know what, we are getting on well, I've got this, I'll answer their questions....." Ring a bell?

Then you blow it, the person doesn't join your business and you are gutted. Or, even worse, you are on the phone with them for an hour and by some miracle they do actually join your business.

"What do you mean even worse?" I hear you mutter.

Well, guess what your new recruit is going to do on every one of their calls? Yep, you got it!

Let's review the world's most simple business building system:

- Write a list of prospects.
- Contact them and have them ask you about your business (whoa that's different!)
- Do not answer their question, instead expose them to a 3rd Party Tool.
- FOLLOW UP and as soon as they ask their first question.....have someone else answer it for you.
- RINSE AND REPEAT

So, now you are saying, that's all well and good, I've heard this a million times, but how do I actually do this? For today's assignment, and I know it is repetitive, contact 5 people, have them ask you about your business, send 'em an email, follow up later in the day and get them on a call with your expert.

"Oh I've tried that before and it didn't work."

We don't recognize the word "try" do we? We don't shirk away from challenges, do we? We don't cherry pick our assignments, do we? No, this Business Builder Book is for people committed to their WHY and committed to do whatever it takes to achieve their WHY.

Name:_____

_____

Email sent:

_____

_____

Follow up:

_____

_____

3 Way Call:

_____

_____

Expert:_____

_____

Outcome:_____

_____

Name:_____

_____

Email sent:

_____

_____

Follow up:

_____

_____

3 Way Call:

_____

_____

Expert:_____

_____

Outcome:_____

_____

Name:_____

_____

Email sent:

_____

_____

Follow up:

_____

_____

3 Way Call:

_____

_____

Expert:_____

_____

Outcome:_____

_____

Name:_____

_____

Email sent:

_____

_____

Follow up:

_____

_____

3 Way Call:

_____

_____

Expert:_____

_____

Outcome:_____

_____

Name:_____

_____

Email sent:

_____

_____

Follow up:

_____

_____

3 Way Call:

_____

_____

Expert:_____

_____

Outcome:_____

_____

# Notes

_____

_____

_____

_____

_____

_____

_____

_____

_____

_____

_____

_____

_____

_____

_____

_____

_____

_____

_____

_____

_____

_____

# DAY 19: FRIDAY REST, RECUPERATE, RECHARGE AND SELFIE TIME!

Usually once a week I give you the day off to rest, recuperate and catch up. For those of you who have completed and posted your selfie, go ahead and take a breather. Those of you who haven't made your selfie debut yet, please complete that today and post it on our Facebook group page.

# DAY 20: SATURDAY
# A TECHNIQUE THAT WILL
# REVOLUTIONIZE HOW YOU
# SPEND MONEY

Legend has it that when a Gurkha warrior pulls his kukuri from its sheath in the heat of combat, he cannot return his knife to the sheath without blood on it. In no way am I comparing us to the most fearsome warriors on the planet. However, as always, there is nothing wrong with being a copycat, so long as you copy the right cats! Where am I going with this?

I have adopted this mentality with my debit/credit card and now, whenever I pull my card out of my wallet to pay for a transaction, I do not return it to its "sheath" until I have approached someone in the vicinity of the transaction, obtained their contact info, scheduled a delivery of a 3rd Party Tool and a follow up. I may approach the person running the card, or someone next to me in line, or a customer at the other end of the room, or someone who walks in before I leave. I do NOT put the card back until I have carried out this little assignment.

It disciplines me, it challenges me and by golly, over the course of a year, it pays for each and every time that card comes out! From now on, no question, you must adopt this strategy. It will absolutely revolutionize your business. Today's assignment is to simply track each time your debit/credit card comes out and to then approach someone. List them below.

**Example:**

Location: Starbucks

Who you approached: Barista

How you approached them: She was mopping up at the end of the night and I approached her regarding our entrepreneur program.

Outcome: She agreed to watch a video if I could send it before she finished mopping. I sent the video and the next morning had confirmation she had watched it.

1. Location:

_____

_____

Who you approached:

_____

_____

How you approached them:

_____

_____

Outcome:_____

_____


2. Location:

_____

_____


Who you approached:

_____

_____


How you approached them:

_____

_____

Outcome:_____

_____


3. Location:

_____

_____


Who you approached:

_____

How you approached them:

_____

_____

Outcome:_____

_____

4. Location:

_____

_____

Who you approached:

_____

_____

How you approached them:

_____

_____

Outcome:_____

_____

# Notes

_____

_____

_____

_____

_____

_____

_____

_____

_____

_____

_____

_____

_____

_____

_____

_____

_____

_____

_____

_____

_____

# DAY 21: SUNDAY
# HOW TO INTRODUCE AND
# EDIFY YOUR EXPERT

Many of you struggle with teeing up the 3 way call correctly so that the prospect wants to listen to your expert. I hear all kinds of beauties such as, "Well, just listen to him for a couple of minutes..." or, "Well, you have to speak to him, that's our system." Even better, "Just let him talk for a couple of minutes then I will come back on the line..."

The key to a successful 3 way call is to correctly present the act of listening to the expert as being a huge benefit to your prospect. The introduction of the idea of getting someone else on the line has to be done in such a way that the prospect is excited and enthusiastic about the opportunity. The first part is to present the reason for getting an expert on the line and the second part is the description or edification of the prospect in a way that appeals to the prospect.

## Exercise 24

Come up with and practice a couple of go-to segues that you can use in all and every situation. Write down 4 and pick the best 2.

**Example:**

"That's a great question and one of the reasons our team does so well is that we have a tremendous amount of experience among the leaders. The best person I know to answer that question would be........"

**Example:**

"Great question, Sally. I just had an idea, the person who answered that question for me was............. She explained it really well and answered my question right away......"

1._____

_____

_____

_____

2._____

_____

_____

_____

3._____

_____

_____

_____

4._____

_____

_____

_____

## Exercise 25

Next, you want to describe your expert using four different categories with one of those four hitting your prospect's hot button. Some prospects want to speak to someone who is FUN. Others want to hear from someone who is proving that they are doing well in the business (FINANCES). A prospect might want to speak to someone who is very knowledgeable (FACTS) and yet another prospect wants to speak to someone who can HELP them.

So there you have it, always describe or edify your expert using those four categories: FUN, FACTS, FINANCES and HELP. No asking of permission, no ickiness, just describing your expert in a way that at least one of those factors will appeal to your prospect. Pick three experts in your company and think about how you would introduce them.

**Example:**

"The best person to answer your question is **Danny**. He is a FUN person, knows all the FACTS about the business, (insert FINANCE tidbit) **he drives a company paid for car** and loves to HELP people."

**Example:**

"That's a great question. One of the reasons why the company is so successful is that we have a lot of very experienced leaders on our team. In fact, the best person I know who could answer your question is **Dale.** He really helped me and explained things very clearly. He's a FUN guy, knows all the FACTS about this opportunity, **picked up a $25,000 bonus just recently** and he loves to HELP people. I don't know if he is available for US, but let's see, hold on."

1. The best person to answer your question is _____. He/she is a FUN person, knows all the FACTS about the business, recently (insert FINANCE tidbit)

_____,

and loves to HELP people.

2. The best person to answer your question is _____. He/she is a FUN person, knows all the

FACTS about the business, recently (insert FINANCE tidbit)

_____,

and loves to HELP people.

3. The best person to answer your question is
_____. He/she is a FUN person, knows all the FACTS about the business, recently (insert FINANCE tidbit)

_____,

and loves to HELP people.

Practice, practice, practice this edification and do not leave anything out! This needs to be so well delivered and it needs to be delivered in a way that makes it of benefit to both you and your prospect. Nail this and you are off to the races!

# Notes

# DAY 22: MONDAY
# HOW TO INVITE SOMEONE
# TO A LIVE EVENT

Many companies provide market parties, launch parties, regionals, etc. It is really important to be able to invite and confirm your guests correctly. Following are some ideas to bear in mind when extending the invitation and setting the correct expectations.

The event will be:

- FUN
- INFORMATIVE
- Opportunity to NETWORK
- Opportunity to MEET NEW PEOPLE
- Will include a BUSINESS PRESENTATION

Do not be apologetic about the business presentation, make it a BENEFIT. And for goodness sake do not set up an AMBUSH! What's an ambush? That's where you invite a friend out and there is either a business presentation thrown in front of them, or you meet them somewhere and "casually" or "coincidentally" you end up at a business presentation. Here goes:

"John, I wanted to invite you to a party I am attending on Tuesday. A bunch of us are getting together at _____. I've been to this kind of party before and I had a blast! That's where I discovered this business that is really changing my life. We need to be there at _____. The presentation starts at _____and we'll be done at_____. We can catch up after the presentation and I will introduce you to some real up and comers, it's always great to meet new people and network isn't it? Cool, see you _____. We are going to have some fun!"

## Exercise 26

Come up with some scripts to invite guests to your next live event. Practice them and refine them until they are natural. Always cover FUN, MEET NEW PEOPLE, NETWORK, PRESENTATION and always remember to tell YOUR STORY.

_____

_____

_____

_____

_____

_____

_____

Next, make sure that you call your guests the day of the event to confirm, or even better, either 3 way someone onto the call to confirm their attendance or simply let your expert have their names and numbers and they can call them to confirm their attendance. The expert says something like this:

"Hi Jody, this is Steve from _____. I am just calling to let you know that I am really excited to meet you tonight at the _____. Andy was telling me what a super sharp person you are, in fact it sounds like you are the kind of person who would be very successful as part of our team. Now, the event is at _____, starting at _____. Do you need me to text you the full address or directions?"

Did you notice I did not call asking to confirm the prospect was coming? I did not call to ask if the prospect had any questions they needed answering. I did not let the prospect have any indication that it was possible to bail out of this event. Be super upbeat, give the prospect a compliment, let them know how much fun it will be. DO NOT mention the company name or its products. Focus only on the event and how much you want to meet them.

**Bonus Tip #3**

Finish off the confirmation call above by asking this simple question and double the number of guests at your parties.

"Oh, by the way, WHO DO YOU KNOW that WE should invite as well?

Cool, what is so special about John?

Great! Let's call him now!"

Hold on a minute, did we just confirm the attendance of a guest and at the same time DOUBLE the number of guests by having the original guest invite someone else? We didn't just DOUBLE the number of people coming to the event did we? Surely it cannot be that simple!!

Today's assignment is to invite 5 people to your next event using the script above.

What 5 people will you invite to your next event?

1. _____

2. _____

3. _____

4. _____

5. _____

On the day of the event, 3 way a call between each guest and your expert who will be at the event to confirm attendance and ask for referrals using Bonus Tip #3.

# Notes

_____

_____

_____

_____

_____

_____

_____

_____

_____

_____

_____

_____

_____

_____

_____

_____

_____

_____

_____

_____

_____

_____

# DAY 23: TUESDAY DOS AND DON'TS FOR LIVE EVENTS

Most companies use live events at convention centers, hotels, restaurants, etc, as recruiting tools. Today we will cover some dos and don'ts when it comes to hosting guests at such events.

Always have someone from your upline call your guests prior to the event to introduce themselves and solidify their attendance at the upcoming event, we covered how to do this in Day 22. On the day of the event, make sure you arrive early and figure out the logistics of the venue. Parking, entrance, where the room is, etc. Scope out the meeting room if possible and plan where you and your guest are going to sit.

Then, give your guest a call and let them know where to park and where to go to meet you. Do not make them figure all this out themselves, they are very "fragile" at this point and any kind of inconvenience may just be enough to turn them away.

Decide who you would like to introduce your guest to either before or after the presentation and why. If possible brief the people in advance and let them know who you will be introducing them to and what you would like them to say or cover in order to help you successfully bring the prospect onto your team.

Decide who you want your guest to avoid meeting and why. You don't want one pissed off member of the company letting off a hand grenade and taking down your guest and anyone in the vicinity with some negative remarks like, "I've been with the company three months and I still haven't got anyone on my team. This stuff is too expensive and my auntie broke out in a rash."

As soon as possible, seat yourself and your guest, get them a glass of water, make sure they are comfortable and have them (and more importantly you) switch off their cell phone. Do not text or look at any social media during the presentation. When the presentation starts, listen intently, act as if this is the first time you have heard this presentation, sit forward in your seat, refer to your guest at poignant moments and basically be excited and enthusiastic about the presentation and the presenter.

When the people delivering their testimonials are wheeled out, if you know any of them and know their stories, let your guest know. This makes the testimonials more real and impactful. Once the presentation is over, you must have a game plan. Decide if you want to have your guest meet anyone else, then move your guest to a suitable area, have the paperwork or your iPad ready and then ask for the order.

Do not ask them if they want to "try" the product or "sample" it, that's just another hurdle you are putting in the way. Realize that immediately after the presentation has been concluded, while there is lots of energy and buzz in the room, this will be the best time ever to ask them to come on board. Do not blow it due to lack of preparation and a game plan.

Today's assignment is for you to put together a game plan for your next event. Plan it and prepare it like a military operation. Plan and prepare for all eventualities. Plan for a successful event in which your prospect joins your team and plan for a not so good outcome where your prospect is still not ready to join you.

List of people invited to the event:

1._____

2._____

3._____

4._____

5._____

6._____

7._____

8._____

Who is going to call them to confirm their attendance?

_____

Will you call them first and 3 way the call, or will they just call them outright?

- Name of Event:
- Location:
- Time
- Do you need to forward directions to your guests?
- Where is the parking and what is the cost?
- What should your guests bring?
- Where and when will you meet them?
- Who do you want your guests to meet?
- Where and when?
- Does the person know you will want them to meet your guests?
- Have you briefed them on what you want them to do?
- How are you going to arrange seating for you and your guests?
- Once the presentation is over, what is your game plan?
- Who do you want your guests to meet immediately after the event?
- Where are you going to usher your guests to?
- How are you going to sign them up? Paper or website?

- If website, do you have the wifi all set up ready to go?

- How are you going to ask them to get started?

- Do you need any help from your team to do this?

- Are you going to need anymore 3rd Party Tools?

- Are you going to allow them to sample the product(s)

- Do you have a special offer or incentive to help them get started right there and then?

- What follow up plans do you have in case your guests are not ready to start right away?

- Do you have a game plan for when your guests sign up right there and then after the event?

- Do you plan on giving them any resources immediately? If so, what, why and how?

Remember, PRIOR PREPARATION AND PLANNING PREVENTS PISS POOR PERFORMANCE. I learned that in the R.A.F. and it is the best way to achieve a successful live event.

By the way, if any of you have any funnies from your past experiences please share them with us on the FB group page. I mean funnies, do not let this turn into a bitching and moaning session. Thank you.

**See Page 95 for a bonus checklist you can complete before each live event.**

# Notes

# DAY 24: WEDNESDAY
# HOW TO FOLLOW UP AFTER A
# 3 WAY CALL

Here we go, on to the next assignment and this is about how to follow up after a 3 way call. Let's recap.

- You've identified a prospect.

- The 5 Second Rule kicked in.

- You referred to your WHY and as a result you decided to approach the prospect.

- You used FORM to build rapport.

- The prospect either asked you what you do or you identified a problem, agitated the problem and then offered a solution.

- You introduced the idea of a 3rd Party Tool and before delivering it you gained an agreement using "If I COULD, WOULD you? WHEN can I? BECAUSE..."

- You then delivered the 3rd Party Tool.

- Next, you followed up at the agreed upon time.

- As soon as your prospect asked a decent question, you edified your expert using FUN, FACTS, FINANCES and HELP.

- You put the expert on the line with your prospect.
- You listened, took notes, and closed out the call as advised by your expert.

Then what? Well, in an ideal scenario the prospect is ready to join your team and has credit card in hand. If so, congrats, sign them up! Often though, the prospect needs some more time and you agreed on a follow up date and time. Now, for that telephone call. Here's how you start it:

"Hi Stephanie, this is Paul with _____. Just checking in regarding our conversation when I introduced you to my friend Josh."

THEN SHUT THE HELL UP.

LISTEN AND TAKE THEIR TEMPERATURE. This is the most important part of the call. By shutting the hell up and listening you will be able to judge just how hot, cold or lukewarm they are.

**Exercise 27**

1. What would a super hot response sound like?

_____

_____

_____

2. What would a super ice cold response sound like?

_____

_____

_____


3. What is a lukewarm kind of temperature sound like?

_____

_____

_____


If their response to your opening is super hot, go straight to the writing up of the order and be ready with the paperwork or be logged in at your back office at the correct page and simply, coolly and calmly walk them through the sign up like you've done this a million times before.

If their temperature is super ice cold, keep your calm, collect your thoughts and find out what happened. Usually if they have gone super cold on you, something or somebody has gotten to them. You need to find out what or who.

"Well, I am sorry to hear that Stephanie, what happened?"

THEN SHUT THE HELL UP.

AND LISTEN.

Don't pounce on their first response. Keep calm and let

them talk. Often their initial response to this question is not the real reason for their change in temperature. So when they deliver their first knee jerk response, let them get it out of their system and then keep silent and silent and silent until they start talking again and that's when they will reveal just what changed their mind.

**Exercise 28**

Can you list the kind of things that can turn a prospect from super hot to super ice cold?

**Example:**

Their brother got to them and told them a story about how a buddy of his joined an MLM, lost money, and now cannot get his car in the garage because of all the excess product he had to buy.

1._____

_____

_____

_____

2._____

_____

_____

_____

3._____

_____

_____

_____

4._____

_____

_____

_____

5._____

_____

_____

_____

What I would do is to re-engage the prospect and have them tell you why their interest was piqued in the first place and just what they were originally interested in (more money, less time away from their kids, new challenge, etc.) You need to get them re-energized again.

THEN SHUT THE HELL UP.

AND LISTEN.

You know the routine by now.

You need to be ready for these responses and temperatures and I will show you how to handle them on another assignment.

Today's assignment is to review the questions above and work on being prepared for all ranges of temperatures when following up after a 3rd party call.

# Notes

_____

_____

_____

_____

_____

_____

_____

_____

_____

_____

_____

_____

_____

_____

_____

_____

_____

_____

_____

_____

_____

_____

# DAY 25: THURSDAY
# ASKING FOR THE ORDER

Here we go, now we are getting down to the business side of things and the "uncomfortable" task of actually asking for the order. Most of you will claim that you are not sales people and don't want to use high pressure sales tactics and I fully understand where you are coming from. HOWEVER, let's get real here. Attending market parties, training, regionals, white parties, mixers, home parties, reading personal development books are all fun and useful, but until you master how to bring on board customers and recruits, you are just kidding yourself and you won't make it.

Ouch.

The fact is, unless you are running credit cards through your back office, you won't get paid. Ouch again! One more time, if you don't learn how to ask for an order, deal with objections and then complete the order you are setting yourself up to fail.

Oh boy, I am hitting you hard. But maybe, just maybe, a hard dose of reality is what you need right now. Sorry, actually, no I am not sorry. There is no way it is possible to turn you into a stone cold closer with one simple assignment. However, you do need to check with yourself just how you feel and how prepared you are when the rubber hits the road and you are about to ask someone to either become a customer or a business partner.

Today's assignment is to simply take a little time and firstly grab the paper sign up forms for customers and business partners and practice filling a couple out. Know the forms inside out, back to front, right to left. Then, go into your back office and do the same. You want your prospect to think you have done this a million times. Write down and practice how you typically ask for the order.

## Exercise 28

What question(s) do you use to ask for the order?

**Example:**

Are you ready to join our team or just be a customer of ours?

1._____

_____

_____

2._____

_____

_____

3._____

_____

_____


Now, write down the typical challenges you have.

**Example:**

_Overcoming the "I can't afford it" objection._

1._____

_____

_____

2._____

_____

_____

3._____

_____

_____

4._____

_____

_____


In the next assignment, I will help you move forward.

# Notes

# DAY 26: FRIDAY
# HOW TO HANDLE
# OBJECTIONS

### DISCLAIMER:

*I cannot teach you how to overcome all objections in one assignment. If I could, I would be a billionaire after having trained the top companies in the world and I would be on a beach right now with a beer in one hand and a blonde in the other.*

However, and you know me by now, I do have a simple formula for you to follow. I did not create this formula, it has been used for years, for good reason. Learn it; master it. Here it is:

**FEEL**

**FELT**

**FOUND**

Simple.

"I understand how you FEEL. In fact many of our team FELT the same way, however, what they FOUND was..."

Notice how I used TEAM and THEY instead of I? We are taking ourselves out of the picture and talking about the TEAM, creating HERD MENTALITY.

**Exercise 30**

Take all your "usual" objections and plug them into the above formula. Don't try and reinvent it, don't cut corners, just apply it to each and every objection you hear.

**Example:**

1. Objection: I don't have the time.

FEEL, FELT, FOUND:

I understand how you FEEL. In fact, many of our team FELT the same way. However, what they FOUND was once they looked at how they use their time, with a little discipline, they could free up 5 hours a week or so.

THEN SHUT THE HELL UP!

1. Objection:

_____

_____

FEEL, FELT, FOUND:

_____

_____

_____

_____

2. Objection:

_____

_____

FEEL, FELT, FOUND:

_____

_____

_____

_____

3. Objection:

_____

_____

FEEL, FELT, FOUND:

_____

_____

_____

_____

4. Objection:

_____

_____

FEEL, FELT, FOUND:

_____

_____

_____

_____

5. Objection:

_____

_____

FEEL, FELT, FOUND:

_____

_____

_____

_____

# Notes

# DAY 27 & 28: SATURDAY AND SUNDAY PUTTING IT INTO PLAY

This weekend I want you to put all you have learned into play as you go about your activities. When you set eyes on a potential prospect, recognize The 5 Second Rule kicking in. Refer to your WHY to motivate you to decide in that 5 seconds to go for it. Create rapport with the prospect using FORM (FAMILY, OCCUPATION, RECREATION and MOTIVATION) and eventually they will ask you what you do.

Answer that question by leading with your WHY..."Before I tell you what I do and how I do it, would you allow me to explain WHY I do what I do?" Once interest has been piqued agree on a 3rd party tool, obtain contact information and set a time for a follow up.

Rinse and Repeat 10 times over the weekend.

List the places you pulled your credit/debit card out over the weekend. For each place, how many prospect names did you get?

1. Location _____

Prospect's Name_____

Follow up_____

Outcome_____

2. Location _____

Prospect's Name_____

Follow up_____

Outcome_____

3. Location _____

Prospect's Name_____

Follow up_____

Outcome_____

4. Location _____

Prospect's Name_____

Follow up_____

Outcome_____

5. Location _____

Prospect's Name_____

Follow up_____

Outcome_____

6. Location _____

Prospect's Name_____

Follow up_____

Outcome_____

7. Location _____

Prospect's Name_____

Follow up_____

Outcome_____

8. Location _____

Prospect's Name_____

Follow up_____

Outcome_____

9. Location _____

Prospect's Name_____

Follow up_____

Outcome_____

10. Location _____

Prospect's Name_____

Follow up_____

Outcome_____


Enjoy the weekend and come back here Monday morning raring to go with at least 10 new prospects. One of those could make you a millionaire!

# Notes

_____

_____

_____

_____

_____

_____

_____

_____

_____

_____

_____

_____

_____

_____

_____

_____

_____

_____

_____

_____

_____

# DAY 29: MONDAY
# TOP AND TAIL

Let's build upon Friday's formula for dealing with all objections.

"I understand how you FEEL. In fact many of our team FELT the same way. But what they FOUND was..."

Let's top and tail it to make it even more powerful. Do not assume that the first objection is the real objection. Generally, the first objection is NOT the real objection and is only a reflex reaction or smoke screen. So, before you dive in to FEEL, FELT, FOUND dig a little deeper. Ask questions to uncover the real objection.

**Exercise 31**

For each objection, write two questions that will help you dig deeper into the initial objection. Peel the layers back, find the real objection and expose it.

**Objection:** "I don't have time."

**Example:** "I hear you, I never have enough hours in the day.

## What kinds of things soak up most of your time?"

1._____

_____

_____

2._____

_____

_____

**Objection:** "I don't have the money."

**Example:** "I hear you, it was rough for me and the family when money was tight, what other sources of income are you looking at?"

1._____

_____

_____

2._____

_____

_____

**Objection:** "I don't like/understand network marketing."

**Example:** "That's common, what kind of things have you heard or experienced when it comes to network marketing?"

1._____

_____

_____

2._____

_____

_____

The message here is to listen for their first objection and then have them clarify it and/or discuss it before you unleash FEEL, FELT, FOUND. That way you can really tailor your use of FEEL, FELT, FOUND to their true objection, therefore making it more powerful. Once you have delivered FEEL, FELT, FOUND it is important to round it out with a benefit and/or interest piquing statement.

So, here it is:

"I understand how you FEEL. In fact many of OUR TEAM FELT the same way. But what THEY FOUND was......AND NOW......."

"I understand how you FEEL, Jeanette. In fact many of the team FELT the same way. But what they FOUND was when they looked at their time over a week, it just took a little bit of discipline to find 4-5 hours for their new business AND NOW they love getting 5 EXTRA PAYCHECKS A MONTH!"

Did you see what I did there? I added the final piece of the

## FORMULA... "AND NOW"

**Example 32**

Write three AND NOW interest piquing statements that you can use to round out your FEEL, FELT, FOUND.

**Example:** <u>AND NOW I have more time to spend with my kids.</u>

1._____

_____

2._____

_____

3._____

_____

**Exercise 33**

Now, let's pull it all together and produce your go to responses for the top 5 "objections" you receive.

**Example:**

Objection: <u>"I have never done sales before."</u>

Question to dig deeper and find out more about the objection:

<u>Oh that is interesting Jeannette, having your own chiropractic</u> <u>practice, how do you actually sign up a new patient? What does</u> <u>that involve?</u>

FEEL, FELT, FOUND statement for this specific objection:

I understand how you feel, in fact many of the medical professional on our team felt the same way. However, what they found was, when they looked at their own practices, what they found was, they were in sales all day long.

AND NOW benefit/interest piquer for this specific objection:

AND NOW, they feel comfortable making recommendations and asking people to become customers.

1. Objection:_____

_____

Question to dig deeper and find out more about the objection:

_____

_____

_____

FEEL, FELT, FOUND statement for this specific objection:

_____

_____

_____

AND NOW benefit/interest piquer for this specific objection:

_____

_____

_____

2.Objection:_____

_____

Question to dig deeper and find out more about the objection:

_____

_____

_____

FEEL, FELT, FOUND statement for this specific objection:

_____

_____

_____

AND NOW benefit/interest piquer for this specific objection:

_____

_____

_____

3.

Objection:_____

_____

Question to dig deeper and find out more about the objection:

_____

_____

_____

FEEL, FELT, FOUND statement for this specific objection:

_____

_____

_____

AND NOW benefit/interest piquer for this specific objection:

_____

_____

_____


4.

Objection:_____

_____

Question to dig deeper and find out more about the objection:

_____

_____

_____

FEEL, FELT, FOUND statement for this specific objection:

_____

_____

_____

AND NOW benefit/interest piquer for this specific objection:

_____

_____

5.

Objection:_____

_____

Question to dig deeper and find out more about the objection:

_____

_____

_____

FEEL, FELT, FOUND statement for this specific objection:

_____

_____

_____

AND NOW benefit/interest piquer for this specific objection:

_____

_____

_____

# Notes

# DAY 30: TUESDAY
# CLOSE OUT THE MONTH
# STRONG

Do not assume.

Do not talk yourself out of contacting someone.

Do not look down your list and miss out a person and go to the next.

Find time today to re-contact with EVERY SINGLE PROSPECT you have spoken to this month.

**Prospects to follow up with:**

1. _____

2. _____

3. _____

4. _____

5. _____

6. _____

7. _____

8. _____

9. _____

10. _____

11. _____

12. _____

13. _____

14. _____

15. _____

16. _____

17. _____

18. _____

19. _____

20. _____

## Exercise 34

Come up with two offers to help them get started as a customer or team member today.

**Example:**

"If you can get started today, not only will you benefit from the company's promotion of a free shake, but I'll also include a free shaker bottle and t-shirt. However, I can only do this extra for 4 people, so please don't miss out."

1. _____

_____

_____

2._____

_____

_____

_____

Gather your team around. Plan how they can finish the month strong and how can you help them. A good exercise is to have each one of them present to you in a way that will convince you to get your credit card out right there. But remember that the system is to 3 way people to you or other leaders in the team. Practice and role play so your team can hit the telephones or get out there Belly to Belly and have a monster finish.

# Notes

# BONUS ASSIGNMENT GOALS, INVENTORY AND PLANNING

Take some time today to review your business. Take inventory of your list. Your list IS the foundation of your business. Is it healthy, thriving, growing organically each day? Or is it stale, dwindling, dying on the vine?

_____

_____

_____

_____

_____

_____

_____

What about you? Are you following Jeff Olson's model of learned knowledge, activity knowledge, learned knowledge, activity knowledge?

_____

_____

_____

_____

_____

_____

_____

_____

What are your strengths?

_____

_____

_____

_____

_____

_____

What are your weaknesses?

_____

_____

_____

_____

_____

_____

What opportunities do you have before you that you can focus on?

_____

_____

_____

_____

_____

_____

_____

What things threaten your business and your success?

_____

_____

_____

_____

_____

_____

What things did you do well last month?

_____

_____

_____

_____

_____

What things could you do better this month?

_____

_____

_____

_____

_____

_____

_____

Mentally, where are you right now?

_____

_____

_____

_____

_____

_____

Are you as excited and motivated as when you just started, or are you getting a little "battle weary?"

_____

_____

_____

_____

_____

When was the last time you wrote down your WHY?

_____

_____

_____

_____

_____

_____

_____

Is your WHY part of your DNA yet?

_____

_____

_____

_____

_____

_____

When you wake up in the morning and think about your business, how do you feel?

_____

_____

_____

_____

_____

How badly do you want this?

_____

_____

_____

_____

_____

_____

_____

Who do you care about most in your team? Who really wants it? Who is putting in the effort?

_____

_____

_____

_____

_____

_____

Do you know how to maximize your compensation plan?

_____

_____

_____

_____

_____

Do you know exactly what each person in your team needs to do to rank advance this month? Do they know and do they have a plan?

_____

_____

_____

_____

_____

_____

How much longer have you given yourself to make this a success?

_____

_____

_____

_____

_____

_____

What alternatives do you have?

_____

_____

_____

_____

_____

---

If you are not as successful as you want to be, can you put your hand on your heart and identify just why not?

_____

_____

_____

_____

_____

_____

_____

What are your goals for this month? Have you written them down? Have you visualized them? Can you see them, feel them, smell them? Are they real? Do you honestly believe you can achieve them this month or are you just going through the motions?

_____

_____

_____

_____

_____

_____

Come on, get real with yourself. Either do this or stop kidding yourself and your family and move on. Do not be a wandering generality, be a meaningful specific.

When people think of you, what do they say? Do they say you are focused and going for it, or do they think that this is just another one of those things you are "trying."

_____

_____

_____

_____

_____

_____

Do you know who you are?

_____

_____

_____

_____

_____

_____

Do you know where you are going?

_____

_____

_____

_____

_____

_____

_____

Do you know how to get there?

_____

_____

_____

_____

_____

_____

What is it going to take for you to fundamentally change? Get your game face on and for the first time in your life be laser focused and finally achieve.

_____

_____

_____

_____

_____

_____

_____

We don't get a second chance. This is not a rehearsal. This is it. This is the opportunity of a lifetime, this is a game changer, this is the vehicle to make it all happen for you and your family. My challenge to you is simple. Take this month and use it as a watershed. Go all out 100% in every possible way you can. No point whatsoever going through the motions, "trying" or "hoping" or "if only-ing." Take inventory, take charge, take no prisoners and grab this opportunity by the scruff of the neck and make this be the month that you look back on in years to come and say, that was the month that changed everything.

# Notes

_____

_____

_____

_____

_____

_____

_____

_____

_____

_____

_____

_____

_____

_____

_____

_____

_____

_____

_____

_____

# LIVE EVENT CHECKLIST

Name of Event:

Location:

Time:

- Do you need to forward directions to your guests?
- Where is the parking and what is the cost?
- What should your guests bring?
- Where and when will you meet them?
- Who do you want your guests to meet?
- Where and when?
- Does the person know you will want them to meet your guests?
- Have you briefed them on what you want them to do?
- How are you going to arrange seating for you and your guests?
- Once the presentation is over, what is your game plan?
- Who do you want your guests to meet immediately after the event?
- Where are you going to usher your guests to?
- How are you going to sign them up? Paper or website?

- If website, do you have the wifi all set up and ready to go?
- How are you going to ask them to get started?
- Do you need any help from your team to do this?
- Are you going to need anymore 3rd Party Tools?
- Are you going to allow them to sample the product(s)
- Do you have a special offer or incentive to help them get started right there and then?
- What follow up plans do you have in case your guests are not ready to start right away?
- Do you have a game plan for when your guests sign up right there and then after the event?
- Do you plan on giving them any resources immediately? If so, what, why and how?

# Notes

# About the Author

Paul G Walmsley has been a proven expert on the telephone for over 13 years. He has honed and mastered his skills as a commission only salesperson earning multiple six figures a year on the telephone. Paul transferred those skills into the world of network marketing and coaches network marketing professionals on the art and science of using the telephone in their home based business. For more information about this workbook and Paul's first book *From HELLO to YES in 3 Minutes or LESS*, along with other helpful tools and resources please visit:

www.mytelephonecoachfreeresources.com